FOOD LOVERS

QUICK & EASY

FOOD LOVERS

QUICK & EASY

RECIPES SELECTED BY ALEKSANDRA MALYSKA AND JONNIE LÉGER

Trans
Atlantic
Press

All recipes serve four people, unless otherwise indicated.

CONTENTS

TOMATO AND BREAD SKEWERS ON PARMA HAM

Ingredients

3–4 thick slices white bread, cut into 1 inch (3 cm) cubes

2 cloves garlic

about ¼ cup / 50 ml olive oil

16 cherry tomatoes

2 sprigs thyme, leaves

6–8 small gherkins

8 slices Parma ham

2 tbsp. extra virgin olive oil

1 tbsp. lemon juice

Salt & coarsely milled pepper

Wooden skewers

Method

Prep and cook time: 15 min

1 Purée the garlic finely with the oil and briefly toss the bread cubes in the flavored oil. Preheat the broiler (grill).

2 Wash and dry the tomatoes and thread on wooden skewers with the bread, alternating tomatoes with bread. Sprinkle with thyme.

3 Cook on all sides under a hot broiler (grill) for about 5 minutes.

4 Drain the gherkins, slice lengthways and put on plates with the Parma ham. Mix the oil with the lemon juice and sprinkle over the gherkins and ham. Arrange the skewers on top and season lightly with pepper and salt. Serve at once.

PORK CHOPS
WITH MUSHROOMS

Ingredients

1–2 tbsp all-purpose (plain) flour

4 boneless pork chops

2 tbsp vegetable oil

For the mushroom sauce:

2 tbsp butter

1 (10-oz) package / 300 g button mushrooms, quartered

1 onion, finely chopped

1 tbsp all-purpose (plain) flour

Scant 1 cup / 200 ml light cream

Salt and freshly ground pepper, to taste

2 tbsp coarse-grained French mustard

1-2 tablespoons milk, as needed

For the vegetables:

Scant cup / 200 ml vegetable broth (stock)

1 lb / 400 g carrots, peeled and cut into matchstick-size pieces

1 cup / 100 g sugar snap peas, trimmed and halved

Method

Prep and cook time: 25 min

1 Spread the flour on a plate. Coat the chops with the flour, shaking off the excess. Heat the oil in a skillet, add the chops and cook until browned and just cooked in the center. Remove from heat and set aside, keeping warm.

2 To prepare the sauce, heat the butter in a skillet; add mushrooms and onion and sauté until soft. Sprinkle with the flour and sauté for 1 minute. Pour in the cream, stirring constantly, and bring to a boil. Season to taste with salt, pepper and mustard. Add milk as needed to thin the sauce. Place the pork chops in the sauce and keep warm over low heat.

3 Meanwhile, bring the vegetable broth (stock) to a boil in a saucepan; add the carrots and simmer, covered, for about 5 minutes. Add the sugar snap peas and simmer 1 minute; drain.

4 Place the pork chops onto plates, spooning mushroom sauce over the top. Serve with the vegetables.

STIR-FRIED VEGETABLES WITH GINGER

Ingredients

2 tbsp oil

1 shallot, chopped

1 tbsp minced garlic

2 tsp minced fresh ginger root

1 tsp salt

2 medium carrots, peeled and chopped into bite-size pieces

½ lb / 200 g asparagus, trimmed and cut into bite-size pieces

½ cup water

½ lb / 200 g bok choy, chopped into bite-size pieces

½ lb / 200 g Napa cabbage (Chinese leaves), chopped

1¼ cups / 200 g broccoli florets

2 tsp sugar

1 tbsp rice wine

1–2 tbsp light soy sauce

2 tsp sesame oil

Method
Prep and cook time: 20 min

1 Heat the oil in a wok and stir-fry the shallot, garlic, ginger and salt for about 1 minute. Add the carrots and asparagus and stir-fry for about 30 seconds. Add the water and cook over high heat for about 2 minutes.

2 Add the bok choy, cabbage, broccoli and sugar; stir in the rice wine and soy sauce. Continue cooking for a further 3 minutes, stirring constantly. Drizzle the sesame oil over the top, divide into bowls and serve immediately.

CHICKEN SATAY WITH GINGER-COCONUT SAUCE

Ingredients

4 chicken legs, skinned

3 tbsp oil, divided

Spice blend (¼ teaspoon each of ground ginger, cayenne pepper, black and white pepper)

2 chili peppers

3 shallots, finely chopped

2 cloves garlic, minced

1 tsp grated fresh ginger root

²⁄₃ cup / 150 ml dry white wine

1 cup / 250 ml unsweetened coconut milk

½ cup (about 125 g) crème fraîche

1 tbsp honey

Freshly ground pepper, to taste

2 tbsp chopped cilantro (coriander leaves)

1 tbsp fish sauce, or to taste

Method

Cook and prep time: 30 min

1 Soak the wooden skewers in enough water to cover them for 15 minutes (to prevent burning).

2 Meanwhile, slice the chicken off the bone and dice. Mix 2 tablespoons of the oil with the spice blend and combine with the chicken. Cover and refrigerate. Preheat the broiler or grill.

3 Wearing gloves to prevent irritation, seed and finely chop the chilies. Heat the rest of the oil in a skillet; add the shallots and garlic and sauté until softened but not browned. Stir in the ginger and chilies; add wine and cook, stirring to loosen bits from the skillet. Boil until reduced, then remove from the heat and add the coconut milk, crème fraîche, honey and ground pepper. Simmer, stirring occasionally, to produce a creamy sauce. Strain through a sieve and add the cilantro (coriander) and fish sauce to taste.

4 Shape the chicken mixture into oblongs, thread onto skewers and broil or grill for 5-6 minutes, turning frequently until cooked through. Arrange on plates and serve with the sauce.

LINGUINE WITH SALMON AND CHEESE-CHIVE SAUCE

Ingredients

14 oz / 400 g linguine

2 tbsp butter, divided

1 onion, finely diced

2 cloves garlic, minced

Scant ½ cup / 100 ml dry white wine

½ cup / 125 ml vegetable broth (stock)

1¼ cups / 150 g grated Gruyère cheese

2/3 cup / 150 g crème fraîche

Salt & freshly ground pepper, to taste

1 hot red chili pepper

1 lb / 450 g salmon fillet, skinned and cut into bite-size chunks

3 tbsp lemon juice

2 tbsp snipped chives

Method

Prep and cook time: 30 min

1 Cook the pasta in boiling salted water until al dente; drain and keep warm.

2 Meanwhile prepare the sauce: heat 1 tablespoon of the butter in a skillet; add onion and garlic and sauté until soft. Add the wine and broth (stock), then stir in the cheese and crème fraîche and simmer for about 5 minutes. Season with salt and pepper and set aside, keeping warm.

3 Wearing gloves to prevent irritation, seed and devein the chili and slice into thin strips. Heat the remaining butter in a skillet and fry the salmon and chili for 2–3 minutes. Season with salt, pepper and lemon juice.

4 Stir the chives into the sauce, toss with the drained pasta and arrange on plates, topped with the salmon.

RISOTTO WITH ZUCCHINI, HAM AND PARMESAN

Ingredients

½ cup / 1 stick /100 g butter

1 onion, finely chopped

1²/₃ cups / 350 g risotto rice

½ cup / 125 ml dry white wine

4 cups / 1 liter beef or chicken broth (stock), hot

2 zucchini (courgettes), trimmed and thinly sliced

4 scallions (spring onions), coarsely chopped

4 tbsp olive oil

¾ cup / 100 g grated Parmesan cheese, divided

1 cup / 150 g chopped air-dried ham

½ bunch basil

Salt & pepper, to taste

Method

Prep and cook time: 30 min

1 Melt half of the butter in a skillet and sauté the onion until soft. Add the rice and stir over the heat until the grains are translucent, about 5 minutes.

2 Stir in the wine and cook until it has evaporated. Then gradually add the hot broth (stock) ½ cup at a time, stirring and adding the next ½ cup when the last addition has been absorbed, until the rice is almost cooked (about 15 minutes).

3 Meanwhile, heat the oil in a skillet and sauté the zucchini (courgettes) and scallions (spring onions) until softened, 3-5 minutes. Set aside.

4 Stir ½ cup of the Parmesan into the risotto and cook, stirring, 5 minutes more, adding a little more broth if necessary. Stir in the rest of the butter, the ham and vegetables into the risotto and season with salt and pepper.

5 Shred half of the basil leaves and stir into the risotto. Spoon the risotto onto plates and garnish with the remaining basil leaves. Top with the remaining Parmesan cheese and serve.

LAMB CHOPS WITH HERB SAUCE AND CHEESE MUFFINS

Ingredients

For the muffins:

2¹/₃ cups / 250 g cups all-purpose (plain) flour

3 tsp baking powder

Pinch salt

1 cup / 100 g shredded American or other processed cheese

1 tbsp finely chopped parsley

1 cup / 250 ml buttermilk

1 egg

2 tbsp vegetable oil

For the lamb and herb sauce:

½ cup / 225 ml olive oil

2 tbsp finely chopped fresh parsley

1 tbsp finely chopped fresh thyme

1 tbsp finely chopped fresh rosemary

3 cloves garlic, crushed

Salt and freshly ground pepper, to taste

12–18 lamb chops (cutlets), trimmed

Method

Prep and cook time: 35 min

1 To prepare the muffins, preheat the oven to 400°F (200°C / Gas Mark 6). Grease a 12-cup muffin pan or line with paper liners.

2 In a medium bowl, combine the flour, baking powder, salt, cheese and parsley. In another bowl, whisk the buttermilk, egg, and oil; pour into the flour mixture and mix just until all dry ingredients are moistened. Pour the mixture into the muffin cups, filling them ²/₃ full. Bake about 20 minutes. Remove from the oven and cool on a rack 5 minutes before turning out.

3 To prepare the lamb, preheat the broiler (grill). Place the oil, parsley, thyme, rosemary, garlic, salt and pepper in a blender and pulse until smooth.

4 Brush the lamb with the herb sauce and broil (grill) until medium-rare, about 3 minutes on each side. Serve with the muffins.

TAGLIATELLE WITH ZUCCHINI, PEAS AND BASIL CREAM

Ingredients

14 oz / 400 g tagliatelle

2 tbsp vegetable oil

1 medium / ¾ lb / 300 g zucchini (courgette), diced

Salt & freshly ground pepper, to taste

Scant ½ cup / 100 ml light whipping cream

Scant 1 cup / 200 ml whole milk

Scant 1 cup / 200 ml chicken broth (stock)

1 bunch basil, leaves separated (reserve a few leaves for garnish)

2 tbsp butter

¼ cup / 30 g all-purpose (plain) flour

1 cup / 150 g frozen peas

¾ cup / 100 g grated Parmesan cheese

1–2 tbsp lemon juice

Method

Prep and cook time: 25 min

1 Cook the pasta in boiling salted water until al dente; drain and keep warm.

2 Meanwhile, heat the oil in a large skillet and sauté the zucchini (courgette) for about 2 minutes. Season with salt and pepper and set aside.

3 In a small bowl, mix the cream, milk and broth (stock). Purée the basil in a blender or food processor with about 5 tablespoons of the cream mixture and set aside.

4 Heat the butter in a medium saucepan over medium heat until foamy; stir in the flour and cook, stirring constantly, for 1-2 minutes without browning. Stir in the rest of the cream mixture and bring to a boil. Add the peas and simmer for about 2 minutes.

5 Stir the cheese into the sauce. Add the diced zucchini, basil purée and lemon juice and season to taste with salt and pepper. Serve with the drained pasta, garnishing with the reserved basil leaves.

TUNA SALAD WITH BAKED TOMATOES

Ingredients

1¼ lb / 600 g small ripe tomatoes, cored and halved horizontally

2 red onions, sliced into wedges

1 dried red chili pepper, seeded and finely chopped (wear gloves to prevent irritation)

Handful finely chopped mixed fresh herbs (try parsley, lemon balm, oregano, rosemary, sage and/or thyme)

5 tbsp olive oil, divided

Salt and freshly ground pepper, to taste

2 (6-oz / 200 g) cans water-packed tuna, drained and flaked

1 bunch arugula (rocket) leaves, trimmed

4 tbsp balsamic vinegar

Method

Prep and cook time: 30 min

1 Place an oven rack 5 inches from the heat; preheat the oven to 500°F (250°C / Gas Mark 9) Line a baking sheet with parchment or foil.

2 Place the tomatoes and onions cut-side-up on the baking sheet. In a small bowl, combine the chili, herbs, and half of the oil. Season with salt and pepper. Sprinkle over the tomatoes and bake until browned, 7–10 minutes.

3 In a small bowl or jar, mix the rest of the oil with the vinegar and season lightly with salt and pepper.

4 Put a bed of arugula (rocket) on each plate. Top with the tuna, tomatoes and onions and serve, sprinkled with the dressing.

SEAFOOD KEBABS

Ingredients

4 large shrimp (prawns), peeled, deveined and halved

8 slices bacon

12 medium scallops

1 lemon, cut into quarters

16 medium shrimp (prawns)

1 lime, cut into eighths

Salt and freshly ground pepper, to taste

Cilantro (coriander) leaves, for garnish

Lemon-flavored oil and/or soy sauce, for dipping

Method
Prep and cook time: 30 min

1 Soak 8 wooden skewers in enough water to cover them for 15minutes (to prevent burning). Preheat the broiler (grill).

2 Wrap each large shrimp with 2 slices of bacon. Thread 2 large bacon-wrapped shrimp, 3 scallops and a lemon quarter onto each of 4 skewers. Take the remaining 4 skewers and alternately thread the medium shrimp and the lime wedges onto each. Season the skewers with salt and pepper.

3 Broil (grill) for about 4 minutes on each side until the shrimp are golden brown. Garnish with cilantro (coriander) and serve with lemon oil and/or soy sauce.

FRIED NOODLES WITH SHRIMP

Ingredients

14 oz / 400 g noodles

3 tbsp. sesame oil

1¾ cups / 200 g sugar snap peas, trimmed

1 red bell pepper, halved, cored and cut into strips

2 cloves garlic, peeled and finely chopped

1 tbsp. sesame seeds

1 chili, deseeded and finely chopped

1 cup / 200 g broccoli florets

2 scallions (spring onions), cut into rings

14 oz / 400 g shrimp (prawns), peeled and deveined

Fish sauce

Method

Prep and cook time: 30 min

1 Cook the noodles in boiling, salted water until al dente, then drain, refresh in cold water and drain well. Keep warm.

2 Heat the oil and sauté the sugar snap peas, bell pepper, garlic, sesame seeds and chili. Then add the rest of the vegetables and stir-fry for 3–4 minutes. Add the noodles and shrimp and stir-fry for a further 2–3 minutes, until all the ingredients are cooked but still have a little bite. Season well with fish sauce and serve.

EGG AND BACON PIE

Ingredients

12 oz (about 300 g) puff pastry,
thawed if frozen

18-oz container / 200 g sour cream

¼ lb /125 g bacon, diced

½ bunch parsley, finely chopped

Hot paprika, to taste

Salt and freshly ground pepper, to taste

4 eggs

Method

Prep and cook time: 40 min

1 Preheat the oven to 400° F (200°C / Gas Mark 6). Grease a 12-inch (30-cm) tart pan.

2 Roll out the pastry into a circle slightly bigger than the tart pan. Line the pan with the pastry, trimming off the excess. Cut out a few decorative shapes from the pastry trimmings. Brush the edge of the pastry with water and decorate with the cut-out shapes, pressing on lightly.

3 Mix the sour cream with the diced bacon, parsley, paprika, salt and pepper; spread onto the pastry, making 4 indentations with a spoon. Carefully break the eggs into the indentations. Bake about 20 minutes, until the eggs are set. Serve immediately.

GREEN BEAN SALAD WITH HALLOUMI CHEESE AND ANCHOVIES

Ingredients

1 lb / 600 g green beans, trimmed

5–6 mild red chili peppers

8–10 oil-packed anchovies, drained

1 head radicchio lettuce, leaves separated

10–12 sage leaves

Juice of 1 lemon

4–5 tbsp olive oil

Salt and freshly ground pepper, to taste

14 oz / 400 g halloumi cheese, sliced*

Method

Prep and cook time: 20 min

1 Bring a large saucepan of salted water to boil. Add the beans and cook until tender-crisp, 8–10 minutes. Drain in a colander under cold running water to stop the cooking; set aside.

2 Meanwhile, preheat the broiler. Wearing gloves to prevent irritation, slice chilies in half lengthwise and remove the seeds; slice into strips. Pat the anchovies dry with a paper towel.

3 Combine the beans, radicchio, chilies, anchovies and sage; drizzle with the lemon juice and olive oil. Season with salt and pepper.

4 Broil (grill) the cheese until golden brown on both sides. Arrange the salad onto plates, place a few slices of cheese on the top and serve.

*Halloumi (or haloumi), from Cyprus, is a semi-soft cheese usually made from goat's and sheep milk; its firm texture makes it suitable for frying or grilling. If unavailable substitute firm mozzarella or feta.

CHICKEN NOODLE SOUP

Ingredients

10 oz / 300 g chicken breast, cut into bite-size pieces

1 tbsp. rice flour, or corn starch (cornflour)

2 tbsp. sesame oil

1 clove garlic, peeled and finely chopped

½ inch / 1 cm piece ginger, peeled and finely chopped

1 tsp. curcuma (turmeric)

4 cups / 1 liter vegetable broth (stock)

1 stick lemongrass, cut into strips

7 oz / 200 g rice noodles

4 scallions (spring onions), cut into rings

1 small Napa cabbage (Chinese leaves), chopped

8 cherry tomatoes, quartered

2 tomatoes, diced

4 tbsp. light soy sauce

4 tbsp. lime juice

Thai basil, to garnish

Method

Prep and cook time: 25 min

1 Mix the chicken pieces and the rice flour in a bowl.

2 Heat the sesame oil in a saucepan and fry the chicken until lightly browned. Add the garlic, ginger, and curcuma (turmeric) and sauté, then pour in the vegetable broth (stock) and bring to a boil.

3 Add the lemongrass to the soup and simmer for about 5 minutes.

4 Put the rice noodles in the soup and simmer for a further 1–2 minutes over a low heat. Add the Napa cabbage (Chinese leaves), scallions (spring onions), cherry tomatoes, and tomatoes and warm thoroughly.

5 Season to taste with soy sauce and lime juice. Garnish with Thai basil and serve.

BRUSCHETTA WITH TOMATOES, OLIVES AND ANCHOVIES

Ingredients

1–1½ baguettes, cut diagonally into slices

2 cloves garlic, halved

1–1½ pints / 500–600 g small cherry tomatoes

Salt and freshly ground pepper, to taste

1 tbsp olive oil

½ small head butterhead lettuce, leaves separated

2 tbsp / 15 g chopped pitted black olives

16-20 anchovy fillets

Method

Prep and cook time: 20 min

1 Rub the baguette slices with the garlic cloves and toast at 400°F (200°C / Gas Mark 6) for about 5 minutes until golden brown. Let cool.

2 Meanwhile, peel the tomatoes: Fill a large bowl with ice water. Bring a large saucepan of water to a boil. Add a handful of the tomatoes and cook 2–3 seconds; quickly remove them with a slotted spoon to the ice water to cool. Repeat with the remaining tomatoes. Drain the tomatoes and slip off the skins. Season with salt and pepper and toss with the oil.

3 Place a few lettuce leaves on the baguette slices, followed by the tomatoes, olives and anchovies.

PENNE WITH POTATOES, CHICKEN AND GREEN BEANS

Ingredients

12 oz / 300 g small new potatoes

½ lb / 250–300 g green beans, trimmed and halved

2 small skinless boneless chicken breasts

Salt and freshly ground pepper, to taste

4 tbsp olive oil, divided

2½ cups / about 11 oz / 300 g penne

1 tbsp finely chopped fresh basil

1 tbsp finely chopped fresh parsley

1 small chunk / about 1 oz / 40-60 g Parmesan cheese

Method

Prep and cook time: 35 min

1 Scrub the potatoes and boil them in a large pan of salted water until cooked. Meanwhile, bring a saucepan of salted water to boil and add the beans and cook until tender-crisp, 8-10 minutes. Drain in a colander under cold running water to stop the cooking; set aside.

2 Season the chicken breasts with salt and pepper. Fry in 1 tablespoon of the oil for about 5 minutes on each side until cooked through, then remove from the skillet. Slice diagonally into strips and keep warm.

3 Cook the penne in boiling salted water until al dente; drain.

4 Meanwhile, heat the remaining oil in a large skillet. Halve boiled potatoes and add them to the skillet along with the green beans and cook, stirring frequently. Season with salt and pepper. Combine with the penne and gently stir in the chicken strips, basil and parsley.

5 Arrange onto plates. Shave Parmesan cheese over the top and serve.

TOMATO SALAD ON TOASTED BREAD

Ingredients

5 tbsp vegetable oil, divided

1 clove garlic, halved

4 large or 8 small baguette slices

2 tbsp balsamic vinegar

1 tbsp lemon juice

1 pinch sugar

1 good pinch dry mustard

Salt and freshly ground pepper, to taste

2 large tomatoes, sliced, halved or quartered according to size

About ½ cup / 100 g / yellow tomatoes

About ½ cup / 100 g red cherry tomatoes

1 stalk celery, thinly sliced

1 red onion, thinly sliced

1 tbsp finely chopped scallion (spring onion) greens

½ cup / 80 g crumbled blue cheese (such as Gorgonzola) or sheep's cheese

Method

Prep and cook time: 20 min

1 Heat 3 tablespoons of the oil in a skillet and sauté the garlic 30 seconds. Remove from the skillet with a slotted spoon and discard. Return the skillet to the heat and fry the bread slices until golden; set aside.

2 In a large bowl, whisk the remaining oil with the vinegar, lemon juice, sugar and mustard, to make a vinaigrette; season with salt and pepper. Add the tomatoes, celery, onion and scallion (spring onion) greens and toss to coat with the dressing.

3 Pile the salad onto the fried bread slices and scatter the cheese over. Serve at once.

FISH SKEWERS ON MIXED SALAD

Ingredients

Juice of 1 lemon

8–12 small fish fillets, such as sea bream, snapper, or arctic char

Salt and freshly ground pepper, to taste

Olive oil, as needed

2 cups arugula (rocket) leaves, trimmed

1 small head radicchio lettuce, leaves separated

2 tomatoes, cut into wedges

4–6 tbsp vinaigrette dressing

Lime wedges, to garnish

Method

Prep and cook time: 25 min

1 Soak 8-12 wooden skewers in enough water to cover for 15 minutes (to prevent burning). Preheat the broiler.

2 Drizzle lemon juice over the fish fillets and season with salt and pepper. Thread the fish onto the skewers. Brush with oil and broil (grill) for about 2–3 minutes on each side.

3 Arrange the arugula, radicchio and tomatoes onto plates, drizzle some of the dressing over the salad and place the fish on the top. Garnish with lime wedges and serve.

SALMON WITH HERBS AND LEMON

Ingredients

1 whole salmon fillet, with skin

Salt, to taste

1 lemon

Scant ¼ cup / 50 ml olive oil

1 small onion, finely chopped

½ bunch parsley, finely chopped

½ bunch basil, finely chopped

⅓ bunch dill, finely chopped

½ inch / 1-cm piece fresh ginger root, peeled and minced

1–2 cloves garlic, minced

Freshly ground pepper, to taste

1 tsp sea salt

Method

Prep and cook time: 25 min

1 Preheat the oven to 400°F (200°C / Gas Mark 6). Grease a long, shallow baking dish (large enough to hold the salmon in a single layer).

2 Lightly salt the salmon. Using a zester or vegetable peeler, zest the lemon and slice into thin slivers. Halve, then juice the lemon into a medium bowl. Add the oil, onion, parsley, basil, dill, ginger, garlic, lemon zest, and pepper.

3 Place the salmon in the baking dish and cover with the lemon-herb mixture. Season with the sea salt. Bake for about 15 minutes or until firm. Serve immediately.

GRILLED SCALLOPS
ON A BED OF GREENS

Ingredients

12–16 medium scallops

Salt and freshly ground pepper, to taste

1 tbsp fresh thyme leaves

About 2 tbsp butter, cut into small pieces

4 tbsp olive oil

2 tbsp balsamic vinegar

6 cups / 200 g mixed salad greens

½ red bell pepper, sliced into strips

½ yellow bell pepper, sliced into strips

Method

Prep and cook time: 15 min

1 Preheat the broiler (grill).

2 Lightly salt and pepper the scallops and place on the broiler tray. Sprinkle a few thyme leaves over the scallops and dot with the butter. Broil (grill) until barely translucent in the center, 3–4 minutes.

3 Meanwhile, whisk the oil and vinegar in a large bowl to make a vinaigrette; season with salt and pepper. Add the salad greens and bell pepper strips and toss to coat.

4 Arrange the salad onto plates, place a few scallops on the top and serve immediately.

STIR-FRIED CHICKEN WITH GINGER

Ingredients

1 lb / 500 g skinless boneless chicken breasts, sliced into strips

1 egg white

1 tbsp all-purpose (plain) flour

1 small hot chili pepper

3 tbsp vegetable oil

2 scallions (spring onions), thinly sliced

1 tsp minced fresh ginger root

1 red bell pepper, diced

2 tbsp rice wine

1-2 tbsp soy sauce

1 tbsp black bean paste

Method

Prep and cook time: 30 min

1 Combine the chicken with the egg white in a medium bowl. Blend the flour to a smooth paste with 2 tablespoons water and mix with the chicken. Wearing gloves to prevent irritation, seed and finely chop the chili.

2 Heat the oil in a large skillet or wok and sauté the chicken until firm. Transfer to a plate and keep warm; return the wok to the heat.

3 Add the scallions (spring onions) and ginger; sauté lightly. Add the bell pepper, chili pepper, wine, soy sauce and bean paste; return the chicken to the wok and stir-fry for a few minutes, until cooked through. Season to taste and serve with rice.

KEDGEREE

Ingredients

2 tbsp vegetable oil

1 small onion, chopped

½ tsp garam masala*

1¼ cups / 300 g long-grain rice

2½ cups / 600 ml fish broth (stock)

½ bunch scallions (spring onions), chopped

12 oz / 300g smoked haddock, flaked

Salt and freshly ground pepper, to taste

¼ cup / ½ stick / 50 g butter, melted

2–3 hard boiled eggs, chopped

4 tbsp chopped fresh parsley

Lemon juice, to taste

Lemon wedges, to garnish

Method

Prep and cook time: 35 min

1 Heat the oil in a large skillet; add the onion and garam masala and sauté until the onion is translucent. Add the rice and continue to sauté for about 1 minute, until the rice grains are well coated. Pour in the fish broth (stock) and bring to a boil; cover and simmer for about 20 minutes or until the rice has absorbed the liquid. Add the scallions (spring onions) and fish about 5 minutes before the end of cooking time.

2 Stir in the butter, chopped eggs and parsley; cook, stirring gently over medium heat for 1–2 minutes. Season to taste with lemon juice, garnish with a few lemon wedges and serve.

*Garam masala, a "warming" spice blend used in Indian cuisine, often contains black pepper, cinnamon, cloves, coriander, cumin, cardamom, fennel and other spices. Find it in Asian groceries and gourmet shops.

PORK CHOPS IN MUSHROOM-MARSALA SAUCE

Ingredients

4 boneless pork chops

2–3 tbsp all-purpose (plain) flour

Salt & freshly ground pepper, to taste

1-2 tbsp vegetable oil, divided

1 lb / about 400 g button mushrooms, sliced

1 onion, finely chopped

1 clove garlic, minced

Scant 1 cup / 200 ml dry Marsala

2/3 cup / about 150 ml beef or chicken broth (stock)

Method

Prep and cook time: 30 min

1 Wash and dry the chops and pound flat. Cut each chop in half. Combine the flour, salt and pepper on a plate; add the chops and coat with the flour mixture, shaking off the excess.

2 Heat the oil in a skillet and fry the mushrooms, onion and garlic in batches until mushrooms are golden brown. Transfer to a plate and keep warm.

3 Return the skillet to the heat, add a little more oil, and fry the chops until golden brown on both sides. Transfer the chops to a plate and keep warm; return the skillet to the heat and add the Marsala. Bring to a boil, stirring to loosen browned bits from the skillet, and cook until reduced slightly. Pour in about half of the broth.

4 Return the pork and vegetables to the skillet, cover and cook over low heat for about 10 minutes, turning the chops occasionally, until the pork is cooked through, the mushrooms are tender, and the sauce is creamy (thin with a little more broth as needed). Season with salt and pepper and serve.

ARTICHOKES WITH MUSTARD DRESSING

Ingredients

4 artichokes

Juice of ½ lemon

For the vinaigrette:

6 tbsp. olive oil

2 tbsp. white wine vinegar

2 tsp. Dijon mustard

1 clove garlic

Sea salt & freshly milled white pepper

Method

Prep and cook time: 40 min

1 Wash the artichokes. Stand the artichokes side by side in a wide pan, half fill with water and add the lemon juice. Put a lid on the pan and cook over a medium heat for 25–30 minutes, until the leaves pull away easily.

2 Peel and finely chop the garlic and crush with 2 pinches of sea salt. Mix with the vinegar, mustard and pepper and whisk in the oil. Season to taste.

3 Drain the artichokes well and serve on plates with a small dish of vinaigrette.

TURKEY AND VEGETABLE STIR-FRY

Ingredients

5–6 tbsp vegetable oil, divided

1 lb / 500 g skinless boneless turkey breast, sliced into thin strips

Salt and freshly ground pepper, to taste

2 large red bell peppers, sliced into strips

2 cloves garlic, minced

2 young thin leeks, thinly sliced (white and light green parts only)

2 tsp. minced fresh ginger root

1 tsp. instant chicken or beef bouillon granules

5–6 tbsp soy sauce

1 cup / about 100 g bean sprouts

2 tbsp. chopped cilantro (coriander) leaves

Method

Prep and cook time: 25 min

1 Heat 2 tablespoons oil in a wok or large skillet over high heat; stir-fry the turkey until cooked through, 2–4 minutes. Season with salt and pepper; transfer to a plate and keep warm.

2 Return the wok to the heat, add the rest of the oil, and stir-fry the bell peppers and garlic 2–3 minutes. Add the leeks, ginger, 5–6 tablespoons water and the broth granules; cover and cook for a further 3 minutes. Stir in the soy sauce and season with salt and pepper.

3 Return the turkey to the wok, add the bean sprouts and heat through. Sprinkle with cilantro (coriander) and serve with rice.

BAKED COD
WITH HERB CRUST

Ingredients

3 slices sturdy white bread

¼ cup / ½ stick / 60 g butter, softened

4 sun-dried tomato halves, finely chopped

1 pinch dried oregano

Salt and freshly ground pepper, to taste

4 cod fillets

2 tbsp lemon juice

1 sprig fresh savory or thyme

12 oz / 35 g green beans, trimmed

½ lb / 200 g snow peas (mangetout), trimmed

Method

Prep and cook time: 40 min

1 Preheat the oven to 350°F (180°C / Gas Mark 4). Line a baking sheet with parchment or foil.

2 Place the bread into a food processor and pulse to fine crumbs. Combine with the softened butter, chopped tomato, oregano, salt and pepper. Sprinkle the fish with lemon juice and spread the crumb mixture on top, pressing to help the crumbs adhere. Place on the prepared baking sheet and bake until firm and topping is well browned, 25–30 minutes.

3 Meanwhile, cook the beans with the savory in boiling salted water for 8–10 minutes, until tender-crisp, adding the snow peas (mangetout) 1–2 minutes before the end of cooking time. Drain, remove the savory and arrange the vegetables on warmed plates. Put the fish fillets on top of the vegetables and serve.

CHICKEN KEBABS WITH COUSCOUS

Ingredients

1½ cups / 250 g couscous

1 cup / 250 ml hot water

3 tbsp butter, room temperature

1 lb / 500 g skinless boneless chicken breasts, cut into wide strips

Salt & freshly ground pepper, to taste

Juice of 1 lemon, divided

1 small zucchini (courgette), finely diced

2 tomatoes, finely diced

1 (14-oz) can / 400 g chickpeas, rinsed and drained

1 bunch parsley, finely chopped

4 radicchio lettuce leaves

Lemon wedges, to garnish

Cherry tomatoes, to garnish

Method

Prep and cook time: 30 min

1 Soak 12 wooden skewers in enough water to cover them for 15 minutes (to prevent burning). Preheat the broiler (grill).

2 Pour the hot water over the couscous and let stand for 10 minutes. Add the butter, stirring it through the couscous with a fork; place over low heat and cook for 5 minutes. Cool.

3 Meanwhile, thread the chicken strips onto the skewers. Season with salt and pepper and sprinkle with lemon juice, reserving 2 tablespoons. Marinate for 10 minutes.

4 Broil (grill) the kebabs about 10 minutes, turning once, until browned and cooked through.

5 Meanwhile, combine the zucchini (courgette), tomatoes, chickpeas and parsley with the couscous; season with salt, pepper and the reserved lemon juice. Fill the radicchio leaves with the salad and arrange on plates with the chicken kebabs and lemon wedges. Garnish with tomatoes.

CRAB SALAD BOATS

Ingredients

8 oz / about 200 g cooked crab meat, picked over to remove shells

1 shallot, finely chopped

2 tbsp mayonnaise

1 tbsp sour cream

4 tsp / 20 ml cognac

Salt and cayenne pepper, to taste

12 large Belgian endive leaves

2 oz / 50 g pistachios, roughly chopped

2 plums, pitted and sliced into thin strips

Method

Prep and cook time: 20 min

1   Mix together the crab meat, shallot, mayonnaise, sour cream and cognac in a bowl. Season with salt and cayenne pepper.

2   Place a spoonful of crab salad onto each endive leaf. Sprinkle each with chopped pistachios, then scatter a few slices of plum on top. Serve immediately.

ASIAN NOODLES WITH PORK

Ingredients

About 1 lb / 400 g Chinese noodles

2 oranges, preferably organic

1 tbsp vegetable oil

1¼ lb / 600 g pork loin, trimmed and cut into thin strips

Scant 1 lb / 400 g sugar snap peas, trimmed

1 orange bell pepper, cored and cut into thin strips

2 red chili peppers, chopped (wear gloves to prevent irritation)

8 scallions (spring onions), trimmed and chopped

½ pint / cherry tomatoes, halved

1 tbsp honey

Light soy sauce, to taste

Method

Prep and cook time: 25 min

1 Put the noodles into a bowl, pour boiling water over them and let stand for about 3 minutes, then drain.

2 Zest the oranges and reserve. Peel the oranges thoroughly and cut out the segments, avoiding the white pith and skin, but catching the juice.

3 Heat the oil in a wok, add the pork and stir-fry until browned. Transfer to a plate, return the wok to the heat and add the sugar snap peas and bell pepper. Stir-fry for about 3 minutes. Then add the chilis and stir in the reserved pork, the noodles, scallions (spring onions), cherry tomatoes and orange segments with the orange juice. Cook for a further 1 – 2 minutes to heat through. Add honey and soy sauce. Serve, sprinkled with orange zest.

CHICKEN SALAD
WITH BEET LEAVES

Ingredients

4 chicken breasts

Olive oil, for frying

Salt & freshly milled pepper

2 cups / 200 g lamb's lettuce

2 cups / 200 g beet (beetroot) leaves

1 yellow bell pepper, deseeded and cut into cubes

2 beefsteak tomatoes, cut into wedges

1 tbsp. coarse Dijon mustard

4 tbsp. olive oil

2 tbsp. cider vinegar

Method

Prep and cook time: 25 min

1 Wash the chicken breasts, pat dry and cut into strips. Heat a little olive oil in a skillet and fry the chicken for about 1–2 minutes on all sides until cooked thoroughly. Season with salt and pepper and place on the side.

2 Wash the lamb's lettuce and beet (beetroot) leaves and shake dry.

3 Make a vinaigrette dressing using the olive oil, cider vinegar, Dijon mustard, and salt and pepper. Place the lamb's lettuce, beetroot leaves, bell pepper, tomatoes and chicken in a bowl, pour in the vinaigrette dressing and toss. Season to taste with salt and pepper and serve.

PENNE WITH TOMATOES AND ASPARAGUS

Ingredients

3½ cups / 400 g penne

1 lb / 500 g green asparagus

1 clove garlic, peeled and finely chopped

4 tbsp. olive oil

1 pinch chili flakes

Scant ½ cup / 100 ml vegetable broth (stock)

1 lb / 500 g plum tomatoes

1 bunch / 75–100 g arugula (rocket)

Salt & freshly milled pepper

Method

Prep and cook time: 30 min

1 Cook the penne in boiling, salted water until al dente.

2 Peel the lower third of each asparagus spear and cut at an angle into pieces about 1 inch (3cm) long.

3 Heat the olive oil and sauté the asparagus with the garlic and chili flakes. Add the vegetable broth (stock), cover and cook for 4–5 minutes.

4 Wash and quarter the tomatoes, removing the hard cores at the top. Add to the asparagus and cook for a further 4–5 minutes. The asparagus should still have a little bite, but the tomatoes should be beginning to collapse.

5 Drain the pasta and add to the vegetables along with the arugula (rocket). Toss to combine, reheat briefly and serve seasoned to taste with salt and pepper.

STUFFED EGGPLANT SLICES

Ingredients

1–2 eggplants (aubergines) sliced lengthwise ½-¾ inch / 1-2 cm thick

Salt, as needed

About 8 oz / 200 g fresh goat cheese

1–2 tbsp chopped fresh herbs of your choice

Salt and freshly ground pepper, to taste

2–3 tbsp olive oil

Lemon juice, for sprinkling

Method

Prep and cook time: 25 min

1 Sprinkle the eggplant (aubergine) slices on both sides with salt. Cover and let stand for at least 10 minutes to draw out some of the water, then rinse and pat the individual slices dry.

2 Meanwhile, mix the goat cheese with the herbs and season with salt and pepper.

3 Heat the oil in a nonstick skillet and quickly sauté the eggplant slices on both sides. Remove from the skillet and sprinkle with lemon juice. Then season with pepper, spread with the herbed cheese and roll up. Serve lukewarm.

POTATO, BEAN AND AVOCADO SALAD

Ingredients

1 lb 6 oz / 600 g salad potatoes

1 lb / 500 g green and yellow beans

4 oz / 100 g bacon, sliced

1 tbsp. oil

2 tbsp. yogurt

1 tbsp. crème fraîche

Juice of 1 lemon

1 pinch sugar

Salt & freshly milled pepper

2 avocados

Dill weed, tips to garnish

Method

Prep and cook time: 40 min

1 Wash the potatoes and steam for about 20 minutes, or until cooked. Leave to cool until lukewarm then halve each potato.

2 Wash and trim the beans and blanch in boiling, salted water for 3–4 minutes until al dente. Refresh in cold water and drain well.

3 Cut the bacon into strips. Heat the oil and fry the bacon until golden brown, then drain on paper towel.

4 Mix the yogurt and crème fraîche smoothly with the lemon juice. Add sugar and salt to taste.

5 Peel and halve the avocados, remove the pits and cut the fruit into wedges. Arrange on 4 plates at once with the other ingredients and sprinkle with the dressing. Season with freshly milled pepper and serve garnished with dill tips.

OMELETTE WRAPS WITH HAM

Ingredients

4 tbsp butter

8 eggs, beaten

½ lb / 200 g thinly sliced ham

Lettuce leaves, thinly sliced

2 medium carrots, peeled and cut into thin strips

Salt and freshly ground pepper, to taste

Method

Prep and cook time: 25 min

1 Heat 1 tablespoon of the butter in an 8-inch (20-cm) nonstick skillet and pour in quarter of the egg mixture, swirling to coat the pan. When the eggs have set, transfer the omelet to a plate and repeat with the remaining butter and eggs to make four omelettes.

2 Arrange the ham, lettuce and carrot strips over the omelettes; season with salt and pepper and roll up to form a wrap. Slice in half along the diagonal and serve.

SHRIMP RISOTTO

Ingredients

1½ tbsp butter

1 tbsp olive oil

1 lb / 500 g shrimp (or prawns), peeled and deveined

1 red onion, finely chopped

1 clove garlic, minced

Heaped 1 cup / 250 g Arborio rice

2/3 cup / 150 ml dry white wine

3 cups / about 750 ml vegetable broth (stock), hot

¾ cup / 100 g frozen fava beans (broad beans)

¾ cup / 100 g frozen peas

2 tbsp crème fraîche

Juice of 1 lime

2 tsp chopped fresh parsley

Salt and freshly ground pepper, to taste

Method

Prep and cook time: 40 min

1 Heat the butter and oil in a large pan; add the shrimp (prawns) and sauté until barely pink; transfer to a plate and set aside.

2 Add the onion and garlic to the pan and sauté for 1–2 minutes. Add the rice and stir until the grains are translucent, about 5 minutes. Stir in the wine and cook until it has evaporated. Then gradually add the hot broth ½ cup at a time, stirring and adding the next ½ cup when the last addition has been absorbed.

3 Add the beans and peas after about 10 minutes, and continue in this way until the rice is soft, 15–20 minutes.

4 Add the crème fraiche, lime juice and parsley; season to taste with salt and pepper and serve.

THAI CHICKEN SALAD

Ingredients

2 green chilies, seeded and chopped (wear gloves to prevent irritation)

1 shallot, thinly sliced

1 tsp shrimp paste

½ tsp. freshly grated ginger root

1 lb / 450 g chicken legs or thighs, skinned, boned, and sliced into strips

8 cups / 400 g mixed salad greens

1 handful cilantro (coriander) leaves

1 handful mint leaves

1 bunch scallions (spring onions), chopped

1 tsp finely grated lemongrass, plus additional slivers to garnish

2 tbsp vegetable oil

1 onion, chopped

2 tomatoes, sliced into wedges

2 tbsp fish sauce

2 tbsp lime juice

1 tbsp brown sugar

Method

Prep and cook time: 20 min

1 Prepare the Thai curry paste: grind the chilies, shallot, shrimp paste and ginger to a paste with a mortar and pestle or in a spice grinder. Transfer to a bowl and add the chicken strips, mixing to coat well.

2 Place the salad greens, cilantro (coriander), mint, scallions and grated lemongrass in a bowl; toss.

3 Heat the oil in a wok or large skillet. Add the chicken and stir-fry about 2 minutes. Transfer to a plate and keep warm. Return the skillet to the heat and add the onion; sauté until soft. Add the tomatoes and cook, stirring briefly.

4 Return the chicken to the wok and heat until cooked through, about 5 minutes. Arrange the chicken, tomatoes and onion on top of the salad.

5 Return the wok to the heat and add the fish sauce, lime juice and sugar. Heat through, stirring to dissolve the sugar, then drizzle over the salad. Serve garnished with lemongrass slivers and herbs.

FETTUCCINI WITH MUSHROOM AND MASCARPONE

Ingredients

14 oz / 400 g fettuccini pasta

2 tbsp butter

1 lb / about 400 g brown mushrooms, trimmed and quartered

2 shallots, finely diced

1 cup / 250 ml vegetable broth (stock)

¼ cup / 50 ml dry white wine

1 cup / 250 g mascarpone cheese

Some fresh thyme leaves, finely chopped (set aside some sprigs for garnish)

Salt and freshly ground pepper, to taste

Freshly grated Parmesan cheese, to garnish

Method

Prep and cook time: 25 min

1 Cook the pasta in boiling salted water until al dente; drain and keep warm.

2 Meanwhile, heat the butter in a large skillet; add the mushrooms and shallots and sauté until tender. Pour in the broth (stock) and wine and simmer for about 5 minutes. Stir in the mascarpone and chopped thyme. Season with salt and pepper.

3 Add the pasta to the skillet and toss with the mushroom sauce to coat and heat through. Divide onto plates, sprinkle with Parmesan cheese, garnish with a sprig of fresh thyme and serve.

SALMON STEAKS WITH HOLLANDAISE SAUCE

Ingredients

For the salmon:

2–3 tbsp lime juice

4 x 7-oz / 200 g salmon fillets

Salt and ground white pepper, to taste

4 tbsp / ½ stick butter, melted

Hollandaise sauce:

1 cup / 2 sticks / 250 g butter

3 egg yolks

Salt and freshly ground pepper, to taste

2 tbsp lemon juice

Fresh dill, to garnish

Thin lime slices, to garnish

Method

Prep and cook time: 30 min

1 Preheat the oven to 375°F (180°C / Gas Mark 5).

2 Drizzle lime juice over the salmon and season with salt and pepper. Pour the butter into a casserole dish. Add the fish, cover with foil, and bake until firm, about 20 minutes.

3 Meanwhile, prepare the hollandaise: melt the butter in a saucepan; skim off and discard the foam. Let cool slightly.

4 Fill a large saucepan ¾ full with water and bring to just below a simmer; set a heatproof bowl over the top. Add the egg yolks and 1 tablespoon of water, whisking until smooth. Slowly add the melted butter, whisking constantly, until creamy. Season to taste with salt, pepper and lemon juice.

5 Pour the hollandaise sauce over the fish; garnish with the dill and lime slices.

SPAGHETTI WITH BACON, WALNUTS, AND GORGONZOLA

Ingredients

14 oz / 400 g spaghetti

1 onion, finely chopped

2 tbsp. nut oil

4 oz / 100 g diced bacon

½ cup / 50 g shelled walnuts

Some fresh parsley

Salt & freshly milled pepper

4 oz / 100 g Gorgonzola cheese

Method

Prep and cook time: 25 min

1 Cook the spaghetti in boiling, salted water until al dente, then refresh in cold water and drain.

2 Heat the oil and fry the onion and bacon until golden brown. Add the walnuts, fry briefly, then add the pasta and fry briefly. Shred the parsley leaves. Add to the pasta and season with pepper and a little salt.

3 Crumble the Gorgonzola over the pasta and serve at once on plates or in bowls.

SHRIMP CAKES WITH SWEET-AND-SOUR SAUCE

Ingredients

1¾ lb / 800 g shrimp (prawns), peeled, deveined, and finely chopped

1 small hot chili pepper

3 cloves garlic, chopped

2 sprigs cilantro (fresh coriander), leaves separated

½ tsp salt

Freshly ground pepper, to taste

1 egg

2 cups / 500 ml neutral-tasting vegetable oil, such as canola or grapeseed

Sweet-and-sour sauce, for dipping

Method

Prep and cook time: 20 min

1 Finely chop the shrimp (prawns). Wearing gloves to prevent irritation, seed and devein the chili and finely chop. Crush the garlic, chili and cilantro (coriander) leaves in a mortar with the salt and pepper. Add the shrimp and blend to a paste. Add the egg and mix well.

2 Form the mixture into approximately 2-inch (5 cm) patties, using 2 tablespoons of the mixture for each one.

3 In a large skillet, heat the oil and fry the shrimp cakes for about 2 minutes, until golden brown. Drain on paper towels. Serve at once with the sweet-and-sour sauce.

GREEN BEANS WITH PARMA HAM

Ingredients
Makes 8 bundles

1 lb 12 oz / 800 g green beans

8 large slices Parma ham

8 thick chives

For the sauce:

1 cup/2 sticks / 250 g butter

2 egg yolks

4 tbsp. dry white wine

2 tbsp. lemon juice

Salt & freshly milled white pepper

Method
Prep and cook time: 30 min

1 Wash and trim the beans and blanch in boiling, salted water for 6-8 minutes, until al dente. Drain in a colander under cold running water to stop the cooking; set aside.

2 Meanwhile make the sauce: clarify the butter by melting it and skimming off the foam. Put the egg yolks and wine into a metal bowl and beat over a pan of simmering water until foamy. Then add the butter, in drops at first, then in a thin stream, beating constantly until you have a creamy, homogenous sauce. The egg yolks must not curdle – don't let it boil! Season with salt and pepper and add lemon juice to taste.

3 Divide the beans into 8 portions, carefully wrap a slice of Parma ham around each bundle and tie with a chive. Serve on warmed plates, pour a little sauce over the bundles and hand the rest of the sauce separately.

PORK CHOPS WITH APPLES

Ingredients

3 tbsp vegetable oil, divided

4 pork chops

½ tsp curry powder

½ tsp honey

Salt and freshly ground pepper, to taste

2 apples, quartered and cut into bite-size chunks

2 red onions, sliced

2 tbsp pine nuts

1 tbsp freshly chopped basil leaves, to garnish

Method

Prep and cook time: 25 min

1 Preheat the oven to 250°F (130°C/ Gas Mark ½).

2 Heat 1 tablespoon of the oil in a nonstick grill skillet and sauté the chops on both sides until brown. Transfer to a baking dish.

3 In a small bowl, mix the curry powder with the honey and 1-2 tablespoons water. Brush the meat with the mixture and season with salt and pepper. Bake for 15-20 minutes, until the meat is just cooked in the center.

4 Meanwhile, add the remaining oil to the skillet, then add the apples, onions and pine nuts and fry all together for 2-3 minutes. Season with salt and pepper.

5 Put the chops on warmed plates, add a little of the apple and onion to each and serve scattered with basil.

GLASS NOODLES WITH CHICKEN AND MINT

Ingredients

2 cups / 200 g glass noodles

3–4 kaffir lime leaves

12 oz / 350 g chicken breast fillet

2 scallions (spring onions)

2 inches / 5 cm ginger, finely chopped

1–2 cloves garlic, finely chopped

3–4 shallots, finely chopped

2 red chilis, deseeded fnd finely chopped (wear gloves)

2 tbsp. / 30 ml sesame oil

2 tbsp brown sugar

Juice of 2 limes

1 small cucumber, peeled and thinly sliced

2 handfuls herbs (mint, cilantro (coriander), Thai basil)

2 limes, halved

1/3 cup / 50 g unsalted peanuts, roasted

Salt & pepper

Method

Prep and cook time: 40 min

1 Soak the glass noodles in lukewarm water and cut into smaller lengths with scissors. In a small pan heat about 4 cups (1 liter) water with the kaffir lime leaves and 1 teaspoon salt. Add the chicken breast and simmer gently over a low heat until cooked (12–15 minutes). Drain, let the meat cool slightly, then tear into small pieces.

2 Drain the glass noodles and cook in salted water, then refresh in cold water and drain well. Peel and shred the scallions (spring onions). Soak in cold water.

3 Heat the oil in a skillet and sauté the ginger, garlic, shallots and chilis for 2–3 minutes. Stir in the sugar, sauté briefly, then add the glass noodles, chicken and lime juice. Season with pepper, mix well and set aside.

4 Drain the scallions and mix them into the chicken and noodles along with the cucumber and herbs. Pile the salad on plates and serve garnished with lime halves and scattered with peanuts.

POTATO PANCAKES

Ingredients

2¼ lb / 1 kg boiling potatoes, peeled and grated

1 onion, finely grated

1 egg

Scant 1 cup / 100 g all-purpose (plain) flour

Salt and freshly ground pepper, to taste

Vegetable oil, for frying

Method

Prep and cook time: 30 min

1 Preheat the oven to a low setting. Line a baking sheet with several layers of paper towels.

2 Spread the grated potatoes and onion on a kitchen towel and roll up jelly-roll (swiss roll) style. Twist towel tightly to wring out as much liquid as possible.

3 Combine the grated potatoes and onion in a bowl. Carefully mix in the egg and flour. Season well with salt and pepper. With your hands, shape into 2-tablespoon mounds, flattening them to form pancakes.

4 Heat about 1 inch (2 cm) of oil in a skillet until hot; add a few pancakes at a time without crowding the pan. Cook on both sides, pressing flat with a spatula, until golden brown. Arrange on the baking sheet and place in the oven to keep warm; repeat with the remaining pancakes. Serve hot.

ZUCCHINI WITH SPINACH, GOAT CHEESE, AND CHICKPEAS

Ingredients

4 tbsp. olive oil

1 tsp. dried thyme

2 zucchini (courgettes), sliced thickly

2 cloves garlic, finely chopped

2 cups / 300 g can chickpeas

3 cups / 300 g baby spinach

1 bunch mint

1 tbsp. capers

Juice of ½ lemon

Sea salt & freshly milled pepper

1½ cups / 200 g goat cheese

Method

Prep and cook time: 40 min

1 Mix the olive oil with the thyme and the garlic. Pour over the zucchini (courgettes) and marinate for about 20 minutes.

2 Remove the zucchini from the oil and place under the broiler (grill) for about 6–8 minutes. Season with salt and pepper. Wash the chickpeas and drain well.

3 Mix the spinach with the mint, chickpeas, and capers and pour the lemon juice and the marinating oil over them. Toss the salad.

4 Season with salt and pepper, sprinkle the crumbled goat cheese over the top, and serve.

Published by Transatlantic Press

First published in 2010

Transatlantic Press
38 Copthorne Road, Croxley Green, Hertfordshire WD3 4AQ

© Transatlantic Press

Images and Recipes by StockFood © The Food Image Agency

Recipes selected by Aleksandra Malyska and Jonnie Léger, StockFood

ISBN 978-1-907176-37-1

Printed in Singapore